D1358460

MISSION TO MARS

MARS MYTHS AND LEGENDS

BY

JOHN HAMILTON

Abdo & Daughters
An imprint of Abdo Publishing | abdopublishing.com

abdopublishing.com

Published by Abdo Publishing, a division of ABDO, PO Box 398166, Minneapolis, Minnesota 55439. Copyright © 2019 by Abdo Consulting Group, Inc. International copyrights reserved in all countries. No part of this book may be reproduced in any form without written permission from the publisher. Abdo & Daughters™ is a trademark and logo of Abdo Publishing.

Printed in the United States of America, North Mankato, Minnesota.
042018
092018

THIS BOOK CONTAINS
RECYCLED MATERIALS

Editor: Sue Hamilton
Copy Editor: Bridget O'Brien
Graphic Design: Sue Hamilton
Cover Design: Candice Keimig and Pakou Moua
Cover Photo: iStock
Interior Images: 20th Century Fox-pgs 39, 42 (inset), 42-43 (*The Martian* film stills); Alamy-pgs 32 & 33; Andy Weir-pgs 39 & 45 (*The Martian* book); AP-pg 15; Doubleday Science Fiction-pgs 38 & 45 (*The Martian Chronicles*); Frank E. Schoonover (artist)-pgs 28 & 29; *Galaxy Science Fiction*-pg 28 (bottom right); Getty-pgs 31 & 44 (Schiaparelli); Henrique Alvim Corrêa-pgs 6 & 25; iStock-pgs 4 & 30 (sound graphic); John Hamilton-pg 11; Library of Congress-pg 44 (Lowell); NASA-pgs 4, 34, 35, 37 & 45 (Mariner 4 & 9 & Face); New York Daily News-pg 45 (Fake Radio Headline); Paramount Pictures-pg 5; PBS-pg 45 (*The Power of Myth*); *Pearson's Magazine*/Warwick Goble (artist)-pg 26; Science Source-pgs 7 & 12-13; Shutterstock-pgs 10, 16, 17, 30 (radio), 36 & 44 (Great Pyramid & Stonehenge); Sidgwick & Jackson-pg 38 (*The Sands of Mars*) *Thrilling Wonder Stories*-pg 28 (bottom middle); U.S. Navy-pgs 18 & 19; University of Michigan-pg 44 (Asaph Hall); Warner Bros-pgs 40 & 41 (Marvin the Martian & *Mars Attacks!*); Wikimedia-pgs 8, 14, 20, 21, 23, 28 (bottom left), 29 (insert), 44 (Mars Statue) & 45 (*War of the Worlds* 1st edition & *A Princess of Mars*).

Library of Congress Control Number: 2017963901
Publisher's Cataloging-in-Publication Data
Names: Hamilton, John, author.
Title: Mars myths and legends / by John Hamilton
Description: Minneapolis, Minnesota : Abdo Publishing, 2019. | Series: Mission to Mars | Includes online resources and index.
Identifiers: ISBN 9781532115943 (lib.bdg.) | ISBN 9781532156878 (ebook)
Subjects: LCSH: Space and time--Juvenile literature. | Mythology--Juvenile literature. | Human-alien encounters--Juvenile literature. | Mars (Planet)--Exploration--Juvenile literature.
Classification: DDC 523.43--dc23

CONTENTS

MYSTERIOUS MARS

Mars,
God
of
War

For much of our history, the planet Mars has represented death and chaos. To the ancient Greeks and Romans, Mars was the god of war, the destroyer. People in early civilizations all over the world looked skyward to that rust-colored point in the sky and trembled. What is it about Mars that frightened them? Even today, when "space invaders" are mentioned, we think of Martians. Invaders from Pluto or Venus just don't seem to terrify us as much. But mention Martians, and you stop a moment, eyes widening maybe just a bit, before you chuckle nervously and move on.

Maybe it's because Mars appears so similar to our own Earth. Both planets have polar ice caps, seasons, and a 24-hour day. It's natural to think there might be some sort of life on Mars. Yet, ancient civilizations knew none of this—to them, Mars was a red-colored point of light in the sky. Why were they so scared?

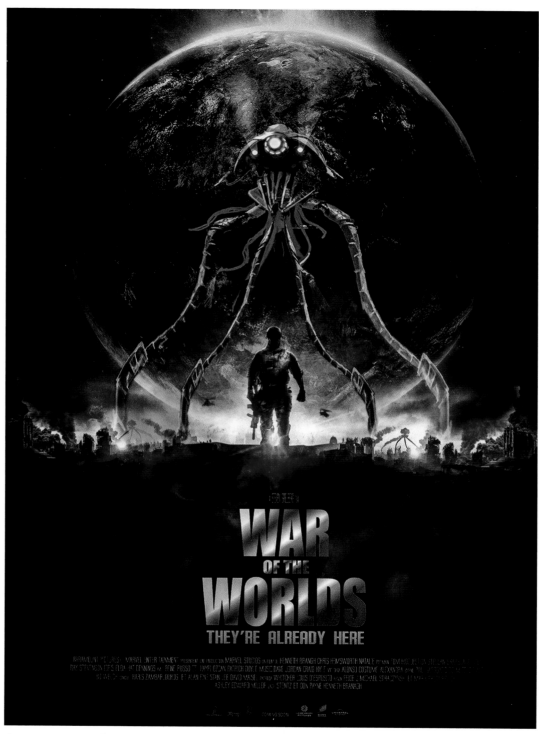

A 2005 poster for *War of the Worlds*, the story of a Martian invasion of Earth.

Mars is part of our culture, our mythology. It has been for thousands of years. Today, in our scientific world, we think everything can be explained. If there's a mystery, we experiment. We analyze the contents of a test tube or peer through a powerful telescope until the problem is solved. But it wasn't always so.

Before the age of science, people still searched for answers to the riddles of nature and human behavior. They turned to myths. The Latin origin of the word myth is *mythos*, a story. Myths give life to society's hopes, dreams, and fears.

An illustration from the 1906 Belgium edition of H.G. Wells's science fiction book, *The War of the Worlds*. In the famous story, Martians arrive and attack Earth. This illustration, by artist Henrique Alvim Corrêa, shows an alien cylinder opening and a Martian emerging to confront a curious and terrified human.

Mars

Mars rises in a clear sky over Ama Dablam, a Himalayan mountain in Nepal. Earthlings have always watched and studied the night sky, wondering, guessing, fearing, and learning what exactly is out there.

Even today, in our scientific society, myths are everywhere. They're often hidden. In *The Power of Myth*, author Joseph Campbell said mythology is "the song of the universe." Myths help us understand characters—called archetypes—such as heroes, villains, shapeshifters, and tricksters.

But what about Mars? How did the Mars myth come to symbolize death and destruction? Why is Mars so frightening? The explanation is there for everyone to see. Go outside on a clear night and gaze upwards. The answer is in the stars.

TRACING THE STARS AND PLANETS

Thousands of years ago, astronomers observed the stars in an effort to understand our place in the universe. The movement of the heavens was reassuringly predictable. The stars always rose in the east and set in the west, just like the Sun and Moon. Stars were arranged in patterns that resembled creatures and objects. We call them constellations today.

A celestial map created by Dutch cartographer Frederik de Wit in the 17th century shows the constellations in the night sky.

The Ensisheim meteorite fell on November 7, 1492. It is the earliest-recorded meteorite. The 280-pound (127-kg) stone landed in a wheat field in Ensisheim, France. At first, pieces of the meteorite were chipped off by souvenir hunters. Today, the meteorite is protected in the town's museum.

The positions of the stars shifted as the seasons changed, but relative to each other, the patterns stayed the same. Sometimes strange lights would flash across the horizon (meteorites), or bright balls with eerie glowing tails hung in the sky for many nights (comets). But these events came and went. Always, the stars remained.

The Greek words meaning "law of the stars" gave us the word astronomy. With the right record keeping, the sky can be used like a calendar. By tracking the predictable star patterns, early astronomers helped people choose the best time to plant and harvest crops, or decide when seasonal herds of animals would pass through their lands. In fact, every advanced civilization of the past, from China to Central America, developed some sort of astronomical knowledge. Most also had religious beliefs connected to their understanding of the heavens.

Many civilizations invented devices, or built structures, to help their astronomers track the stars. In Egypt, the Great Pyramid of Giza is aligned to the polestar (Polaris, the North Star). Seasons are tracked by the position of the pyramid's shadow. A temple built by the ancient Anasazi people in Chaco Canyon, New Mexico, has a window through which a shaft of sunlight enters and covers a special spot on the opposite wall only on June 21, the summer solstice (the longest day of the year). Stonehenge, a circular formation of huge stone slabs in England, was built about 4,500 years ago. It accurately predicted the positions of the Sun and Moon, and the changing seasons.

Stonehenge is circle of huge stone slabs in Wiltshire, England. It may have been built for religious ceremonies or as a kind of early planetarium. No one knows who built the ancient circle of rocks, but the prehistoric monument began construction about 4,500 years ago. Other monuments in the area are even older.

The Sumerians, the Babylonians, Egyptians, as well as the Mayans and Aztecs of Central America, all developed accurate calendars and almanacs based on the regular movement of the stars. Navigation aids were also invented that relied on predictable star patterns.

However, five lights in the night sky acted strangely. Today, we know that these are the five planets that can be seen without a telescope: Mercury, Venus, Mars, Jupiter, and Saturn. To ancient people, these

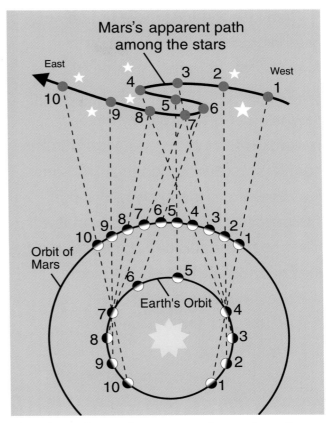

This chart shows the retrograde motion of the planet Mars. Because Earth moves faster around the Sun, Mars appears to backtrack (points 4, 5, and 6) before resuming its west-to-east movement through the zodiac.

"stars" wandered through the sky. One night a star might be near the constellation of Scorpius, but a few weeks later shift positions to Sagittarius or Capricornus. (In fact, the word "planet" comes from the Greek *planetes*, which means "wanderers.") Sometimes, these strange lights even moved backward for a short time, or looped, before continuing their eastward movement through the string of constellations (the zodiac). Astronomers call this backward movement *retrograde motion*.

Predictable things make us feel safe, like we're in control. We grow fearful when an unpredictable event happens. When ancient astronomers saw wandering stars, they were naturally filled with dread. Maybe some sort of disaster was looming. (*Disaster* is a Greek word meaning "bad star.") Astronomers could track the planets through the night sky, but they couldn't explain their complicated movements.

When there is a gap between our understanding and the way things are, myth fills the space. That is why we gave the planets human traits. It was an attempt to make sense of the unexplainable. The planets became supernatural—they were gods that lived in the heavens.

There was one planet that troubled astronomers most of all. Its light never flickered like a star, and it glowed an ominous red color. Its movement through the sky was the most erratic of the planets. It was the least predictable, and the most frightening. That planet was Mars, the god of war.

A view of the Alaskan night sky with a glowing green aurora borealis, stars, and planets. Ancient astronomers tried to understand the difference between the stars and the planets. When their knowledge failed them, myths filled in the gaps.

MARS IN GREEK AND ROMAN MYTHOLOGY

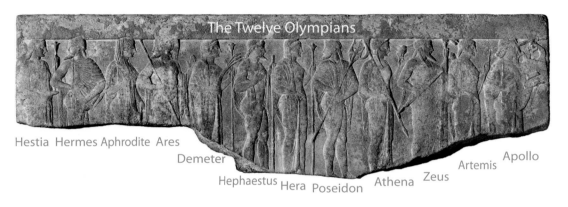

The Twelve Olympians

Hestia Hermes Aphrodite Ares

Demeter

Hephaestus Hera Poseidon Athena Zeus

Artemis Apollo

About 3,000 years ago, the ancient Greeks believed in many gods. The twelve Olympians were the most powerful. They were the controllers of natural forces such as the wind, the oceans, and earthquakes. The five known planets were each named after different gods, depending on how they moved in the heavens. For example, Mercury, having the swiftest path through the zodiac, was named after Hermes, the quick messenger of the gods. Mars was named Ares, the god of war, because of its unpredictable, unusual motion. Later, during the ancient Roman period, the planet was called as we know it today—Mars.

Much of ancient Greek culture was passed down to modern Western civilization. Like the ancient Greeks, today we value reason and logic, fairness, and a curiosity of the natural world. The opposite of the Greek ideal is war—fighting, murder, and disorder. Mars the planet represented all these bad traits as Ares, the god of war.

Hipparchus, a Greek astronomer, maps the stars in ancient Egypt.

15

Greek cults sprang up in which Ares was worshipped, especially in the city-state of Sparta. Later, in ancient Rome, Ares became known as Mars. The cult of Mars became even stronger, with Roman citizens believing that Mars was their protector. Ancient Rome was a conquering society, where war and conflict were common. And as the Romans invaded other lands, so spread the cult of Mars.

Myths are powerful forces in civilizations. They teach us how to behave in society, or how not to behave. Our myths are passed down from generation to generation until their messages are assumed to be "the truth." We believe them without question. That's why, even to this day, when we think of Mars, we think of negative things that our society fears and hates. Because of our Greek heritage, Mars will always be looked on with suspicion and fear.

Ares, God of War

The Temple of Ares
in Athens, Greece.

SCHIAPARELLI AND THE MARTIAN CANALS

During the late 1800s, better telescopes opened the skies to fresh observations. It was during this time that astronomers discovered that Earth's Moon was a dead, crater-filled place. There was no life to be found on our nearest neighbor.

If the Moon was dead, then the next best place to look for extraterrestrial life might be the planet Mars. But even with the largest, most advanced telescopes available at the time, the Red Planet was difficult to observe. Faint polar caps of ice could be seen. Large splotches of blue-green color was mixed with the reddish Martian soil. Astronomers wondered if these splotches could be oceans, or maybe even vegetation, since they seemed to change size with the seasons.

Astronomer Asaph Hall

Astronomers kept their telescopes trained on Mars, searching for more signs of life. In 1877, the orbits of Mars and Earth brought them closer together than they had been in many years, making for very clear observations. That year, American astronomer Asaph Hall, using the 26-inch (66-cm) telescope at the U.S. Naval Observatory in Washington, DC, discovered the existence of Mars's two moons, Phobos and Deimos.

The 26-inch (66-cm) refractor telescope at the U.S. Naval Observatory in Washington, DC. In 1877, Asaph Hall discovered the two moons of Mars using this telescope.

Astronomer Giovanni Schiaparelli was the director of the Brera Observatory in Milan, Italy. During his long career, he made many discoveries and observations, especially of comets and meteors. But in 1877, with his 8-inch (20-cm) telescope focused on Mars, Schiaparelli announced a discovery that changed the way we think of the Red Planet.

Schiaparelli had very sharp eyesight. It was a valuable trait for astronomers during this time, before photography was widely used with telescopes. Using his superior vision, Schiaparelli drew maps of Mars that included what he thought were oceans and continents. Then, in 1877, Schiaparelli saw enormous lines crisscrossing the planet.

Astronomer Giovanni Schiaparelli

At first, the astronomer doubted his own discovery. Mars was hard to see at that time, even with the best telescopes. But night after night, Schiaparelli saw these lines, which he called *canali*. It is an Italian word that means "channels" or "grooves."

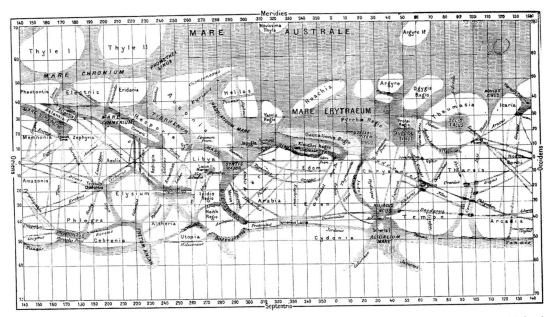

Italian astronomer Giovanni Schiaparelli mapped Mars from 1877 to 1886. Aided by his telescope and sharp eyes, his map included *canali*, channels or grooves on the planet. Many people misunderstood and thought the "canals" were dug by intelligent life on Mars. Decades passed before that concept was proven false.

In the 1960s and 1970s, when NASA sent its Mariner missions to Mars, scientists discovered a 3,000-mile (4,828-km) -long canyon called Valles Marineris. Did Schiaparelli see Valles Marineris all the way back in 1877? We may never know. Some scientists today explain his observations as optical illusions. But whatever he saw, his announcement caused a worldwide sensation.

Many people misunderstood Schiaparelli's use of the Italian term *canali*. They thought the astronomer had observed "canals" on Mars. It was proof, they believed, that there was intelligent life on the Red Planet. Some people said that the Martians must have dug the canals to bring melting water from the polar ice caps to help the rest of the thirsty, desert planet.

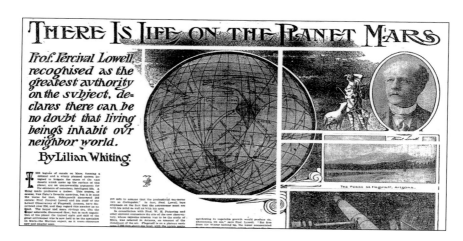

Astronomer Percival Lowell believed there was life on Mars.

A few years before Schiaparelli's discovery, in 1869, the Suez Canal had been completed in Egypt. It was a technological marvel for its time, and only proved to people that these canal-building Martians must have a very advanced civilization. Schiaparelli was more cautious about his discoveries. He believed there was probably a natural explanation for the lines he was seeing on Mars. He kept searching for more clues until his failing eyesight forced him to stop in 1892.

The news of the Martian "canals" caused many people to point their telescopes toward the Red Planet. Percival Lowell, who in 1894 built a large observatory on a mountain near Flagstaff, Arizona, was certain that the canals were real. He spent many years observing Mars and searching for life. He wrote three popular books on the subject. His enthusiasm fueled the public's imagination.

This popular belief of life on Mars led to an explosion of stories about the Red Planet. In these early science-fiction tales, authors tried to guess what kind of superior beings lived on Mars. Most agreed that the Martians had to be smarter and wiser than humans.

Then, in 1897, British author H. G. Wells published a novel that forever changed how we think of Martians.

Percival Lowell sits at his telescope in his Flagstaff, Arizona, observatory.

THE WAR OF THE WORLDS

H.G. Wells

Herbert George (H.G.) Wells was an English author. He was most famous for his science-fiction novels. He wrote more than 80 books, including *The Time Machine* in 1895, and *The Invisible Man* in 1897.

During the end of the 1800s, people were alarmed that Germany was strengthening its army and navy. Many countries feared a German invasion. Wells used this fear, plus the horror of modern weapons and technology, as themes in his new novel, *The War of the Worlds*.

The story was first published in parts in *Pearson's Magazine* in 1897. It was then published as a novel in 1898. *The War of the Worlds* is a classic alien invasion story. Martians flee their dying world and land on Earth in giant cylinder-shaped rockets. Using huge "fighting machines" (pods on long metal legs), they begin their invasion by attacking London, England. Their weapons are "heat rays" and toxic black smoke. The citizens of Earth are helpless against the Martian technology. Then, the aliens drop dead. They had no natural defense against the simplest of Earth creatures: germs.

A Martian fighting machine attacks in an illustrated 1906 edition of H.G. Wells's *The War of the Worlds*.

Artwork from *The War of the Worlds* published in 1897.

The War of the Worlds begins ominously. An unknown threat appears to be coming from Mars. Following is a section of the novel's famous opening paragraph:

"No one would have believed in the last years of the nineteenth century that this world was being watched keenly and closely by intelligences greater than man's. . . that as men busied themselves about their various concerns they were scrutinized and studied, perhaps almost as narrowly as a man with a microscope might scrutinize creatures that swarm and multiply in a drop of water. . . No one gave a thought to the older worlds of space as sources of human danger. . . Yet across the gulf of space, minds that are to our minds as ours are to those of the beasts that perish, intellects vast and cool and unsympathetic regarded this Earth with envious eyes, and slowly and surely drew their plans against us. . ."

Some people compare the events in H.G. Wells's *The War of the Worlds* to Europe's invasion of Tasmania in the 1700s. Many natives were killed in warfare or from diseases brought by the Europeans.

When H.G. Wells created *The War of the Worlds*, he did more than write an alien invasion story. He also criticized British society. At the time Wells wrote the novel, Great Britain was busy invading countries all over the world and turning them into colonies. Some people compare the events in *The War of the Worlds* to Europe's invasion of Tasmania. Great Britain began settling the island in the late 1700s. In the years that followed, many native Tasmanians were either killed in warfare or died from diseases brought by the Europeans. Tasmania today is a state of Australia.

*The War of the World*s was also about one of Wells's favorite themes—survival of the fittest. A clear example happens at the end of the novel, when the seemingly invincible invaders are killed off by simple Earth bacteria.

The War of the Worlds was a huge success for H.G. Wells. It came out during a time of great public interest in Mars. The book had a big impact on our culture. Alien invasion stories remain popular to this day.

For 30 years after the publication of The War of the Worlds, a great many stories and books about Mars were written. They fed the public's imagination. Edgar Rice Burroughs, author of the Tarzan of the Apes stories, wrote a series of popular books about Mars (called "Barsoom"), starting in 1917 with A Princess of Mars. These books told of the adventures of John Carter. He was a swashbuckling hero who overcame Martian warriors with the use of sword and magic.

In 1938, there was a fictional story that had an even bigger impact on how we look at Mars, and it didn't come on the printed page. It was told on a relatively new medium, one with an untested power to sway the public imagination: radio.

Many stories about Mars and Martians came out in the 20th century.

Edgar Rice Burroughs wrote a series of adventure books about the heroic John Carter on Mars, beginning in 1917 with *A Princess of Mars*.

THE PANIC BROADCAST

On October 30, 1938, Halloween eve, America was treated to a prank. That night, a CBS Radio play based on H.G. Wells's *The War of the Worlds* was broadcast. Written by Howard Koch, it featured 23-year-old director and actor Orson Welles and The Mercury Theatre on the Air.

The play began with a mock broadcast from a hotel in New York City. It featured a live performance by Ramon Raquello and his orchestra. The music was interrupted by fake news reports of Martians landing in the small New Jersey town of Grovers Mill. The invaders soon opened fire with their "heat rays." The Martians destroyed everything in their path, including New York City. Some of the fake news reports were modeled after the famous 1937 Hindenburg airship disaster radio broadcast. Together with realistic sound effects and riveting narration, the play was thrilling.

In fact, for many people it was *too* thrilling.

In 1938, most Americans heard daily news reports of war from Latin America and Asia. Nazi Germany controlled much of Europe. The public was already suffering from "war jitters." It didn't seem so far-fetched that invaders from Mars could land on American soil.

Radio listeners on October 30, 1938, heard Orson Welles report that there were "explosions occurring on the Planet Mars." Later in the program, he stated that a "huge, flaming object" had fallen to Earth on a farm near Grovers Mill, New Jersey. More landings were soon reported and a frightened radio audience concluded that Earth was under invasion by Martians.

When *The War of the Worlds* was broadcast, panic swept the nervous nation. Many people tuned in their radios too late to hear Welles introduce the fictional play. As many as one million people actually believed Earth was being invaded by Martians. Some terrified citizens rushed out into the streets, or even fled the cities. Local legend says a shotgun-wielding farmer shot at a water tower in Grovers Mill. He had mistaken it that dark night for a Martian fighting machine.

William Dock was ready to hold off Martians at his farm by Grovers Mill, New Jersey. In 1938, about 4 to 6 million people listened to *The War of the Worlds* broadcast. Around 1.7 million of those people thought it was a real invasion, with 70 percent saying they were frightened.

The panic broadcast doesn't make much sense today. The entire play lasted just 45 minutes. That was not enough time to blast off from Mars, travel 35 million miles (56 million km) through space, and then conquer the entire Earth. That so many people were fooled proved how powerful the new technologies of radio and other mass media could be.

Orson Welles was stunned by the public's reaction. He later told reporters that he had been unsure whether to perform the play at all. "It was our thought," he said, "that people might be bored or annoyed at hearing a tale so improbable."

At the start of The Mercury Theatre on the Air's next regular broadcast, Welles apologized for the panic. But the play made Welles famous. He went on to Hollywood to direct film classics such as *Citizen Kane* and *The Magnificent Ambersons*. Still, it was the panic broadcast of 1938 for which many will remember Welles.

A monument was erected in Grovers Mill, New Jersey, on the 50th anniversary of the 1938 *The War of the Worlds* panic broadcast.

THE FACE OF CYDONIA

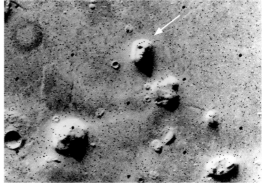

In 1976, the Viking 1 orbiter sent back a photo of Mars that seemed to show a huge human face (see arrow) looking back from Mars's Cydonia region. The speckled appearance of the image is due to missing data, called bit errors, caused by problems transmitting photographic data from Mars to Earth. Bit errors comprise part of one of the "eyes" and "nostrils" on the eroded rock mesa. Shadows in the formation give the illusion of a nose and mouth.

During the summer of 1976, the Viking 1 orbiter was busy taking photographs of the surface of Mars. During one of its orbits, the spacecraft passed over the flat plains of Cydonia. It is a region in the northern hemisphere of the planet. NASA scientists were surprised when they saw an image beamed back to Earth. Staring back at the camera was a huge, humanoid face. It had a nose, eyes, and even a mouth.

The "Face" on Mars is an eroded rock formation. It measures about 1.5 miles (2.4 km) long, 1.25 miles (2.0 km) wide, and .25 miles (.4 km) tall. When it was first discovered, scientists dismissed it as a trick of lighting. Shadows in the rocks give the illusion of facial features.

The Face was not the only unusual feature seen in Cydonia. Several other curious structures were found in the same area. They included what looked like pyramids. There was also a structure that looked like the ruins of an ancient city, or fortress.

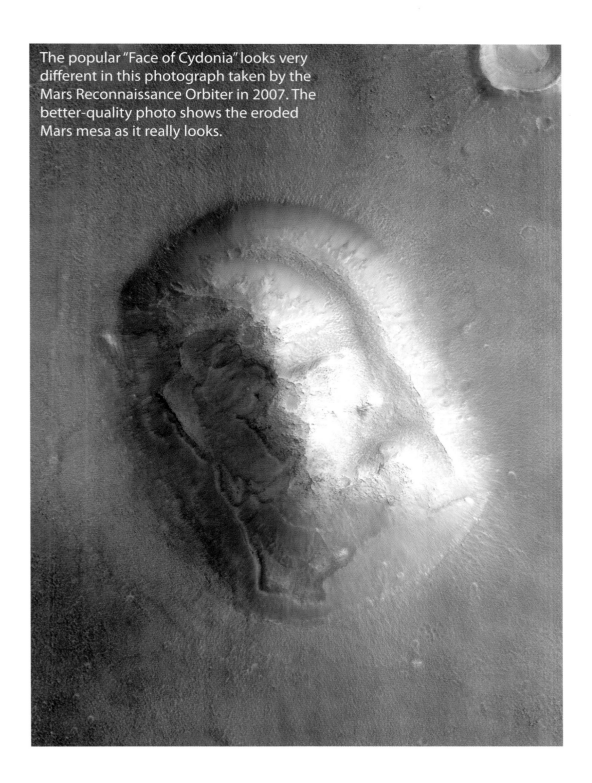

The popular "Face of Cydonia" looks very different in this photograph taken by the Mars Reconnaissance Orbiter in 2007. The better-quality photo shows the eroded Mars mesa as it really looks.

NASA scientists were sure these structures, including the Face, were unusually shaped rocks and hills, like mesas in the American Southwest. They released the photo to the public. NASA thought it would be an interesting curiosity. Little did they realize what a sensation it would cause.

Starting in 1977, the Face of Cydonia became a hot topic. Many people were sure that the Face proved the existence of a past civilization on Mars. Several books presented wild theories about its origins. Some believed a long-dead race of Martians left the Face behind. It was a monument to their civilization, just like the pyramids of the ancient Egyptians. Other people were convinced NASA was covering up the truth about the Face.

Some people believed a long-dead race of Martians left behind monuments to their civilization on Mars.

Scientists said it was all nonsense. The Face, the pyramids, and the fortress are just rock formations. The Face looks like a human because of a coincidence in lighting and natural erosion. We know that on Mars there is wind and probably seismic activity (marsquakes). We also know that in the planet's ancient past, running water eroded the landscape.

NASA's Mars Global Surveyor spacecraft arrived in Mars orbit in 1997. The probe took photos of the Martian surface that were ten times sharper than the Viking 1 orbiter of 1976. When scientists received the new images, they saw… rock formations, just as they had predicted. There was not a single alien in sight.

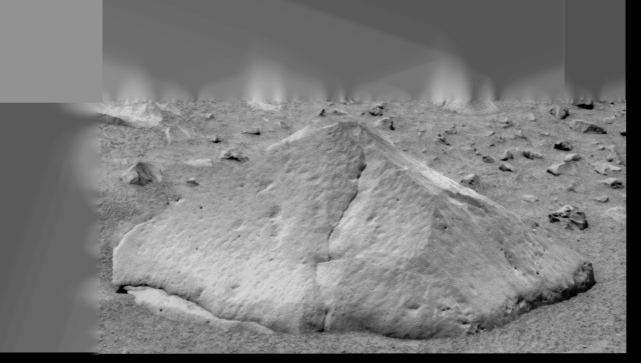

Above is a close-up view of what some people thought might be a pyramid. Nicknamed "Adirondack" (after the Adirondack mountains in New York), the rock's size and dust-free surface made it the first destination for the Mars rover, Spirit, in 2004. The expanded view (below) shows that the rock is only about the size of a football. It is naturally formed and *not* a Martian-made pyramid.

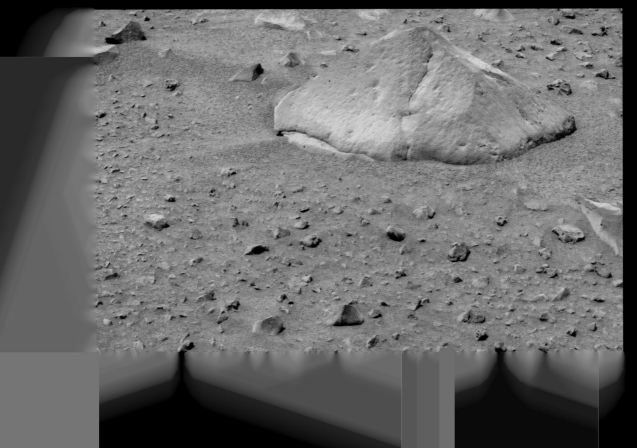

MARS IN POPULAR CULTURE

In the mid-1900s, authors continued to write stories about Mars. Ray Bradbury gave the subject a new spin with his masterpiece, *The Martian Chronicles*. First published in 1951, it is a collection of short stories that record the human colonization of Mars. Instead of Martians conquering Earth, it's humans who invade the Red Planet. Martians have died out, but somehow continue to haunt the human visitors. The aliens

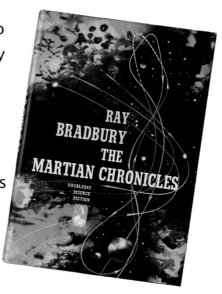

in *The Martian Chronicles* are wise and peaceful. That is unlike many of the humans who settle on the planet. In the end, it's the Earthlings who become the new Martians.

In *The Sands of Mars* (1951), by Arthur C. Clarke, a writer visits a colony on Mars and discovers native life forms. Another science-fiction classic about Mars is Robert Heinlein's *Stranger in a Strange Land*. It won the Hugo Award in 1962.

Starting in the 1960s, a series of NASA Mariner spacecraft proved that Mars was a cratered, desert planet. It was hostile to life. Writers began crafting stories that showed this new reality. Many stories were about Earthlings colonizing and terraforming Mars. Some of the most popular modern books include *The Martian Race* (1999) by Gregory Benford; *Mars* (1992) by Ben Bova; and *Red Mars* (1993) by Kim Stanley Robinson (plus its two sequels, *Green Mars* (1993) and *Blue Mars* (1996)).

In 2011, author Andy Weir published *The Martian*. It has sold more than 3 million copies. That makes it one of the most popular books about Mars in recent times.

Andy Weir's *The Martian* has sold more than 3 million copies. It was made into a movie in 2015 starring Matt Damon.

People have always had a huge appetite for movies and television shows about Mars. Dozens of films have been made about Mars or Martians since the 1950s. Some of the most popular include *Invaders From Mars* (1953), *War of the Worlds* (both the 1953 version and Steven Spielberg's 2005 film), *Total Recall* (1990) starring Arnold Schwarzenegger, and *Mars Attacks!* (1996) by director Tim Burton. Some movies were strictly for laughs, including Disney's *RocketMan* (1997). Even Bugs Bunny got in on the act. In 1948, Loony Tunes introduced Marvin the Martian.

With his Roman centurion's helmet, deadly ray gun, and plans to blow up Earth, Marvin was a worthy opponent for that "wascally wabbit" Bugs.

The Expanse is a popular television series based on the Hugo Award-nominated book series by James S. A. Corey. It takes place 200 years in the future. People from Earth have colonized Mars and the nearby asteroid belt. A delicate peace is shattered as each side tries to dominate the solar system and the galaxy beyond.

Marvin the Martian

In 2016, the National Geographic Channel began a docudrama called *Mars*. The miniseries combines interviews with real-life experts with a fictional story set in the year 2033. In season one, the first astronauts to set foot on Mars accidentally land far from their base. The astronauts must struggle against the harsh Martian landscape as they journey to safety.

Matt Damon played astronaut Mark Watney in the 2015 movie, *The Martian*. Director Ridley Scott brought Andy Weir's novel to life, realistically showing the efforts of a stranded astronaut (Damon) to survive on Mars.

In 2015, director Ridley Scott brought Andy Weir's 2011 novel *The Martian* to life on the big screen. Like the book, the movie followed astronaut Mark Watney's struggle to survive being stranded on Mars. Both the book and film are hailed for their devotion to realism. Despite his grim situation, Watney retains his humor, and uses his knowledge of science to make his survival and rescue possible. The outdoor scenes in *The Martian* were filmed at Wadi Rum, in southern Jordan. The red sand and stark rock outcroppings closely resemble the landscape on Mars.

The power of myth to influence our feelings about Mars has been affecting our culture for thousands of years. Perhaps someday, when humans are firmly established on Mars, we'll lose our fear and dread of the Red Planet. But in the meantime, the myth lives on.

As Orson Welles said at the end of *The War of the Worlds* panic broadcast in 1938, "So good-bye everybody, and remember, please, . . . the terrible lesson you learned tonight. That grinning, glowing, globular invader of your living room is an inhabitant of the pumpkin patch, and if your doorbell rings and nobody's there, that was no Martian. . . it's Hallowe'en."

TIMELINE

Great Pyramid of Giza

2560 BC—The Great Pyramid of Giza, also known as the Pyramid of Cheops, finishes construction by the Egyptians. Its north-south axis is aligned with the North Star.

Stonehenge

2500 BC—Prehistoric people in today's England finish construction of Stonehenge, a collection of huge standing stones arranged in a circle. The site may have been used as a burial ground, and to predict the position of the Sun and Moon.

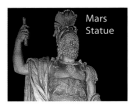
Mars Statue

500 BC—Classical Greek civilization begins. The ancient Greeks believe in many gods, including Ares, the god of war. The ancient Romans later called Ares as we know him today—Mars.

Giovanni Schiaparelli

1877—Italian astronomer Giovanni Schiaparelli draws first detailed map of Mars. He sees long, straight lines on the planet, which he calls canali.

Asaph Hall

1877—American astronomer Asaph Hall discovers the two Martian moons, Phobos and Deimos.

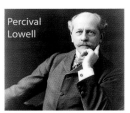
Percival Lowell

1895-1908—American astronomer Percival Lowell publishes a series of books and includes detailed drawings of the Martian "canals" (which later prove to be optical illusions). Lowell's books convince many people that intelligent life resides on Mars.

1897—*The War of the Worlds*, by English author H.G. Wells, first published.

1917—*A Princess of Mars*, by American author Edgar Rice Burroughs, first published.

Oct. 30, 1938—Orson Welles's *The War of the Worlds* radio broadcast causes widespread panic.

1951—*The Martian Chronicles*, by American author Ray Bradbury, published.

July 14-15, 1965—Mariner 4 (USA) spacecraft, first successful flyby of Mars.

Nov. 14, 1971—Mariner 9 (USA) orbiter arrives at Mars. First United States spacecraft to orbit a planet other than Earth.

1976—NASA's Viking 1 orbiter takes images of a strange, face-like rock formation on the Martian region of Cydonia.

1988—PBS first broadcasts *The Power of Myth*, a series that features Joseph Campbell, the writer who popularized character archetypes and mythology.

2011—*The Martian,* by America author Andy Weir, published.

GLOSSARY

ASTEROID

A rocky object, smaller than a planet, that revolves around the Sun, usually between the orbits of Mars and Jupiter. Their size ranges from one to several hundred miles in diameter. Mars's two moons, Phobos and Deimos, are probably asteroids captured by the planet's gravitational pull millions of years ago.

CULT

A religious group that especially worships a special person, goal, or even an object. In ancient Roman culture, the cult of Mars became popular as the Roman army invaded other lands.

EXTRATERRESTRIAL LIFE

Life that does not come from the planet Earth, popularly called alien life. It might range from simple germs to complex, intelligent organisms. So far, extraterrestrial life has not yet been discovered. Many experiments on Mars have been conducted in order to find out if extraterrestrial life may once have lived on the Red Planet.

NATIONAL AERONAUTICS AND SPACE ADMINISTRATION (NASA)

A United States government space agency started in 1958. NASA's goals include space exploration, as well as increasing people's understanding of Earth, our solar system, and the universe.

OLYMPIANS

Major gods of ancient Greek culture. They lived atop Mount Olympus. The 12 Olympians included Aphrodite, Apollo, Ares, Artemis, Athena, Demeter, Hestia, Hephaestus, Hera, Hermes, Poseidon, and Zeus. Ares, the god of war, would later come to be called Mars by the ancient Romans.

ORBIT

The circular path a moon or spacecraft makes when traveling around a planet or other large celestial body. There are several satellites orbiting Mars, including NASA's Mars Reconnaissance Orbiter and the European Space Agency's ExoMars Trace Gas Orbiter.

PROBE

An unmanned space vehicle that is sent on missions that are too dangerous, or would take too long, for human astronauts to accomplish. Probes are equipped with many scientific instruments, like cameras and radiation detectors. Information from these instruments is radioed back to ground controllers on Earth.

TELESCOPE

A device to detect and observe distant objects by their reflection or emission of various kinds of electromagnetic radiation (like light). Most astronomy instruments today detect electromagnetic radiation other than visible light, such as radio or x-ray telescopes.

TERRAFORM

Modifying a planet on purpose to make its atmosphere, temperature, and ecology similar to Earth's. The dream of some scientists is to terraform Mars so that large populations of colonists from Earth can someday live on the Red Planet.

ONLINE RESOURCES

Booklinks
NONFICTION NETWORK
FREE! ONLINE NONFICTION RESOURCES

To learn more about Mars myths and legends, visit abdobooklinks.com. These links are routinely monitored and updated to provide the most current information available.

INDEX